This notebook belongs to...

....

centum

Published 2013. Century Books Ltd.
Unit 1, Upside Station Building Solsbro Road,
Torquay, Devon, UK, TQ26FD

books@centurybooksltd.co.uk

Distributed in the USA and Australia by DK
345 Hudson Street, New York, NY 10014, USA
707 Collins Street, Melbourne,Victoria 3008, Australia
English language exports distributed by DK
80 Strand, London, WC2R 0RL
001-197401-July/13

I ♥ 1D

CONTENTS

This Is Me...

Name:

Age: Birthday:

Star sign:

Address:

Email:

Hair colour: Eye colour:

Height:

Signature:

My favourite things:

My favourite 1D songs:

Stick in a pic!

This pic was taken:

7

THEN AND NOW!

Wow! So much can happen in just a few years. From living in separate places all over the UK, to meeting up and making new best friends and then conquering the world – the One Direction journey so far has been amazing!

When I first saw them, I thought ....

....

I loved .... the most.

Now when I look at them, I think .... Now I love .... the most.

flirt photogenic funny sensible giggly

'It's amazing to think back to when we were first put together – and to the point we are at now. Things have moved so quickly, it's got all of us in a massive state of shock. It's so surreal to think of everything – like winning the BRIT, doing our first UK tour, having our first number one. I can't believe all of this has happened to us five lucky guys. We love our fans and owe all our success entirely to them – we want them to know that.' Liam

9

HARRY STYLES

Gorgeous and multi-talented Harry is the youngest in the band. Not only does he speak French and play the kazoo, he can also juggle – a very useful talent for someone with so much going on! He even came up with the name, One Direction. Rumour is that he doesn't get why girls find him so attractive... ummmm... it's quite obvious to everyone else!!!

I ♥ HARRY

Fact File:
Name: *Harry Styles*
Birthday: *1st February 1994*
Star Sign: *Aquarius*
Height: *178cm (5ft 10)*
Eye colour: *Green*
Born in: *Holmes Chapel, Cheshire, England*
Twitter: *@Harry_Styles*

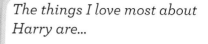

The things I love most about Harry are...

....

....

....

....

....

....

....

'A dream is only a dream until you decide to make it real.' *Harry.*

LIAM PAYNE

Lovely Liam is a big romantic with a secret talent for beatboxing. He says that he's too shy to flirt, but that only adds to his charm. His nickname is Daddy Directioner as he is the most mature in the group and more than 6 million people want to read his sweet tweets!

I ♥ LIAM

The things I love most about Liam are...

....

....

....

....

....

....

....

Fact File:
Name: *Liam Payne*
Birthday: *29th August 1993*
Star Sign: *Virgo*
Height: *178cm (5ft 10)*
Eye colour: *Brown*
Born in: *Wolverhampton, West Midlands, England*
Twitter: *@Real_Liam_Payne*

'Dreams are like stars — you may never touch them, but if you follow them, they will lead you to your destination.' *Liam.*

ZAYN MALIK

This lovable lad has loads of cool talents including being able to draw and play the triangle. Although he can't swim and is scared of the dark, his sensitive side only makes us love him more!

I ♥ ZAYN

14

Fact File:
Name: *Zayn Malik*
Birthday: *12th January 1993*
Star Sign: *Capricorn*
Height: *175cm (5ft 9)*
Eye colour: *Light brown*
Born in: *Bradford, West Yorkshire, England*
Twitter: *@ZaynMalik*

The things I love most about Zayn are...

....
....
....
....
....
....
....

'Life is a funny thing, the minute you think you've got everything figured out something comes along and turns it all upside down.'

Zayn.

NIALL HORAN

Gorgeous blonde Niall is the only band member not born in England. Proud to support his Irish heritage, he has the colours of his country's flag stuck to the bottom of his microphone. Rumour is it that he never went to his school prom – probably because too many girls wanted to go with him lol! Niall usually signs his tweets with kisses ... awwww!!!

I ♥ NIALL

Fact File:
Name: *Niall Horan*
Birthday: *13th September 1993*
Star Sign: *Virgo*
Height: *171cm (5ft 7)*
Eye colour: *Blue*
Born in: *Mullingar,*
County Westmeath, Ireland
Twitter: *@NiallOfficial*

The things I love most about Niall are...

....
....
....
....
....
....
....

'Being single doesn't mean you're weak, it means you're strong enough to wait for what you deserve.' Niall.

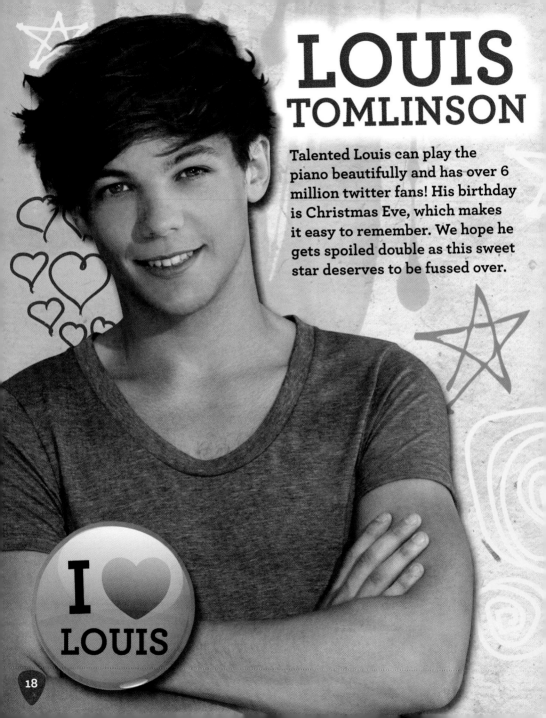

LOUIS
TOMLINSON

Talented Louis can play the piano beautifully and has over 6 million twitter fans! His birthday is Christmas Eve, which makes it easy to remember. We hope he gets spoiled double as this sweet star deserves to be fussed over.

I ♥ LOUIS

Fact File:
Name: *Louis Tomlinson*
Birthday: *24th December 1991*
Star Sign: *Capricorn*
Height: *175cm (5ft 9)*
Eye colour: *Blue*
Born in: *Doncaster,*
South Yorkshire, England
Twitter: *@Louis_Tomlinson*

The things I love most about Louis are...

....

....

....

....

....

....

....

'The fact that we can make people happy from what we love doing is incredible.' Louis.

AMAZING
ALBUM DEBUT

One Direction's debut album, *Up All Night*, went to number 1 in 17 countries! Wow, what a success story!

The album was recorded in Sweden, the UK and the US. The boys loved working with some of the world's best writers and producers. Released in the UK and Ireland in Autumn 2011 and worldwide in 2012, this awesome album has sold more than 3 million copies so far!

In the mix...

Check your answers on page 92

1. Which song was written by Kelly Clarkson?

2. Can you name the tracks that were released as singles?

3. How many tracks are there on the album?

'I want people to listen to it and say, "Wow, is that One Direction?". It's not too cheesy – I think it's the kind of album that guys will like as well as girls.' Louis.

ONE DIRECTION
TAKE ME HOME

WE LOVE THE 2ND ALBUM!!!
xxx

SENSATIONAL SINGLE DEBUT

The boys' debut single, *What Makes You Beautiful*, was released on 11th of September 2011 in the UK and was #1 in UK and Ireland. This massive hit broke the record for most pre-orders in Sony's history. The first single, *Live While We're Young*, from their second album is on track to blitz that record!

'To think we've sold the most number of pre-orders when you know some of the artists who have released records through Sony is incredible! We can't believe it. It's the most amazing thing,' Zayn.

Enter Via Door:2

The 'Up All Night' tour sold out all 60 shows in the UK and Ireland. When they won their first BRIT award for Best Single... it was time for a 1D World Tour.

ONE DIRECTION
WHAT MAKES YOU BEAUTIFUL

As soon as it was available in iTunes, *What Makes You Beautiful* was #1 in the UK and Ireland. It went on to sell 153,000 in the first week! A phenomenal success.

The video was super successful as well – it has more than 1/4 billion hits on YouTube and counting!

ONE DIRECTION
One Direction Presents
ONE DIRECTION
PLUS SPECIAL GUESTS
(VIP) FRONT ROW
Enter Via Door:2
56780753547

ONE DIRECTION

A78

1D

MY SONG

A song is like a musical poem and comes from the heart.
Write about something that is important to you.

My song is about:

Title:

Verse 1

Chorus

I ♥ HARRY - ZAYN -

I ♥ ONE DIRECTION

Verse 2

Verse 3

Verse 4

NIAll — LOUIS & LIAM

AND THE AWARD GOES TO...

Here are some of their wins!

BRIT Award for Best Single 2012:
What Makes You Beautiful

Nickelodeon Kids' Choice Awards 2012:
Favourite UK Band, Favourite UK Newcomer

MTV Video Music Awards:
Best Pop Video, Best New Artist, Most Share-Worthy Video

Teen Choice Awards:
Choice Music: Breakout Group,
Choice Summer Music Star: Group,
Choice Music: Love Song for What Makes You Beautiful

4Music Video Honours:
Best Breakthrough, Best Group,
Best Video What Makes You Beautiful

Other 1D wins:

- First UK group to debut at No. 1 in the USA
- *What Makes You Beautiful* was the biggest pre-order single in history for Sony
- This first single hit #1 in the UK and Irish charts as soon as it was on iTunes
- It also debuted at #28 on the Billboard Hot 100
- The album *Up All Night* entered the US Billboard 200 chart at #1

What total stars!!!!

The award I would give them is ....
Because ....
....

WHAT MAKES YOU BEAUTIFUL

It's so true that often some of the most beautiful things about people are qualities that they don't see in themselves. Looking for the best in people around you is a great quality to have.

Some of the beautiful things that I love about my bffs that they sometimes don't see in themselves are:

Name: _____ is beautiful because _____ .

Name: _____ is beautiful because _____ .

Name: _____ is beautiful because _____ .

Name: _____ is beautiful because _____ .

Name: _____ is beautiful because _____ .

Make sure you often tell your besties how beautiful they are rather than just think it. Positive energy is best when it's shared around – the more the better!

This is a pic of my beautiful friends!

Some good things people say about me that I find it hard to see in myself are:

You can ask your mum or a trusted friend to help you out with this one! It can be really hard, but there will be lots of beautiful things about yourself once you think about it. Make sure that you remind yourself of your good qualities, too.

I ♥ ONE DIRECTION

SWEET TWEETS

Awww we love hearing from the 1D boys themselves! Here are some of the best...

@Harry_Styles
The difference between doing something and not doing something is doing something.

@NiallOfficial
This is gona be such a fun year, take me home is coming out and we're goin on the #TMHtour

@Louis_Tomlinson
Little unknown fact I'm 1/16 Belgian.

@Real_Liam_Payne
I wish I was Iron Man.

@zaynmalik
Thankyou for today guys, you lot are incredible for getting us here. Love you all :)

I ♥ 1D

My fav 1D tweets are...

....

....

....

....

....

I'm following...

AWESOME TOUR EXPERIENCES

When the boys released their first single in the UK it was hard to keep their feet on the ground!

Harry and the boys were so excited to be signing copies of their very first single. It was a dream come true!

Australian Directioners could not get enough of their fav boys, lining up for hours just to get a glimpse.

These lucky girls got to take the boys home with them lol!

Their UK home tour saw them performing in front of thousands of fans.

The boys deliver another awesome performance at the MTV Music Awards in Los Angeles.

One Direction performed at the 62nd Sanremo Music Festival in Italy to loads of adoring fans.

In Paris, France, fans swamped the Virgin Megastore Champs-Élysées to get to see One Direction!

ONE DIRECTION

WORDSEARCH

Find the words below in the grid and circle them. Words can be found vertically, horizontally and diagonally, both forwards and backwards.

AWARDS
BAND
BEAUTIFUL
BOYS
DIRECTIONER
FAME
FRIENDS

FUN
HARRY
LIAM
LOUIS
LOVE
MOMENTS
NIALL

ONETHING
POP
SUCCESS
TAKEN
XFACTOR
ZAYN

Check your answers on page 92.

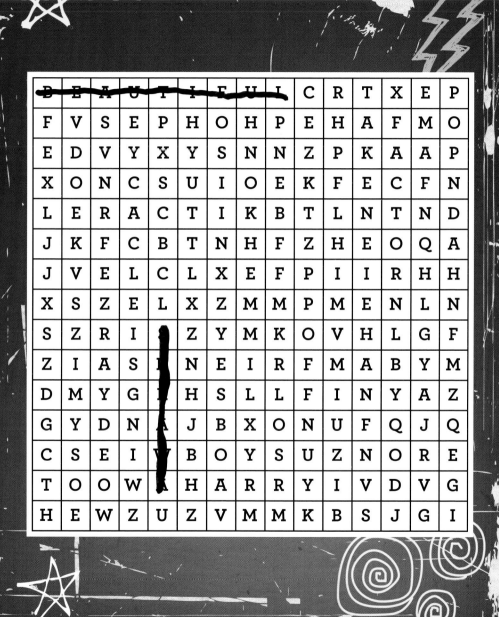

ONE DIRECTION
WORDPLAY

How many words can you make from

ONE DIRECTION

1. nice

5 words – you're doing ok!

10 words – good work!

15 words – what a star!

Check your answers on page 92.

39

Fan Fiction

Writing great fan fiction just takes a big dose of imagination and splash of talent! Think of a scene with the boys and how it might pan out. Once you've polished your story, think about uploading it to a One Direction fan fiction site. It can be great to get good feedback from other writers!

Are You A True Directioner?

Here are some quick questions to brush up on your band knowledge. Once you've taken the test, see if your friends are as 1D smart as you are!

I ♥ ONE DIRECTION

Quick Quiz

1. Which band members have the middle name 'James'?
2. Who came up with the bands' name?
3. Who was in a band called White Eskimo?
4. Which song on Up All Night was written by Kelly Clarkson?
5. Who hates it when people chew with their mouth open?
6. Zayn means 'beautiful' in which language?
7. Which ear does Zayn have pierced?
8. What is Harry's middle name?

ONE DIRECTION

Multiple Choice...

1. Harry signs his name:
a) Harry ✔
b) Hary
c) Haz

2. Zayn's middle name is:
a) Javadd ✔
b) David
c) James

3. Harry's star tattoo has:
a) five points
b) six points
c) seven points ✔

4. Louis and Harry first met:
a) onstage at X Factor ✔
b) in the toilets at X Factor
c) in line at X Factor

5. Zayn's name was originally spelled:
a) Zane
b) Zain
c) Zayne ✔

6. Whose middle name is William?
a) Louis ✔
b) Harry
c) Zayn

7. When Zayn mimed 'Hello' through a car window to a fan, she:
a) screamed
b) mimed 'I love you' back ✗
c) passed out

43

My 1D Short Story

Get your smarts on and create your own 1D story! What would happen if you met? Where would you meet? Remember the who, what, where, when and why of storytelling. Write one story or a few really short ones. It's all up to you.

I ♥ ONE DIRECTION

If you're stuck for inspiration, use interesting facts about people to trigger your imagination. For example, Louis has said that if he had a superpower, it would be flying, and Liam said he would want to be invisible! Imagine what would happen if they did have those superpowers!

I ♥ ONE DIRECTION

My 1D Short Story

SUPERSTAR STYLIN'

Whether they are playing to the crowd on stage, or just hanging out together relaxing, the boys always look great!

All of the boys love their fashion! They easily mix designer threads and mainstream favourites to create their sharp stage looks.

ONE DIRECTION

One Direction Presents

ONE DIRECTION

PLUS SPECIAL

Even just hanging out between performances and appearances they still know how to throw a hot look together.

BEFORE THE FAME

It's hard to imagine the boys before X Factor rocketed them to interstellar stardom and they became the boys we know and love! What will the mags write about what you and your bffs were up to before fame came knocking at your door?

My fav hobbies:

I was studying/working:

My pet peeve was:

My bffs were:

Before we were famous we loved:

Now that we're famous:

Harry

- Was studying to become a lawyer – he's super-smart and gorgeous!
- Worked part-time at the W. Mandeville Bakery in his home town when he was 16
- When he was lead singer for White Eskimo they won a Battle of the Bands. Once a star, always a star!

Niall

- Has played guitar as long as he can remember
- Used to perform all over his homeland
- Loved geography in school.

Louis

- Was a waiter at a Vue Cinema and at Doncaster Rovers soccer stadium
- Has been a musical star in many productions, including playing Danny Zuko in Grease at high school
- Was in a UK drama called If I Had You.

Liam

- Studied music technology at City of Wolverhampton College
- Used to be a member of the Scouting Association
- Performed at a Wolverhampton Wanderers' soccer match
- Auditioned for X Factor in 2008, but Simon Cowell told him to come back in two years.

Zayn

- Didn't have a passport
- Had never been on a plane
- Wanted to get an English degree and become a teacher.

BACKSTAGE PASS

VIP PASS
1D
ONE DIRECTION

Celeb spotting alert! The boys got snapped in 2011 in London at Heart Radio's annual Have A Heart Appeal fundraising day.

Fun photo opp! Messing around backstage at the *What Makes You Beautiful* launch.

Which song does each of these mixed-up lyrics belong to?

11. me can't want you now that you have me suddenly

12. cause heart race make be can't brave ever you my I

13. out head my of so out get get out get

14. replay replay she's on Katy Perry

15. no try I hard how right can't ever get it matter

16. you're what don't for know insecure

17. fun say too but wanna young all we we're have is they that

18. being you're I know don't why shy

19. screwed listen never mess tell me I I'm a up that

Check your answers on page 93.

SECRET CRUSH

They are all so crush-worthy and each has their own particular charm. But which of the boys is your fav and why?

I 🖤 _____ *the most.*

Because...

I ♥ ONE DIRECTION

I ♥ ONE DIRECTION

stick a pic here!

I ♥ HARRY

Lush!

I ♥ ZAYN

Harry

stick a pic here!

Delish!

stick a pic here!

stick a pic here!

I ♥ LOUIS

ONE DIRECTION

I ♥ LIAM

ONE DIRECTION
One Direction Presents
ONE DIRECTION
PLUS SPECIAL GUESTS
(VIP) FRONT ROW
Enter Via Door:2
56780753547
1D
A78

I ♥ 1D

I ♥ NIALL

MY BEST BAND MOMENTS

There are just so many cute sayings and adorable things that they do, that it's really hard to pick favourites!

It was so funny when...

I loved it when...

It's really nice when they...

You could tell they really care about each other when...

I thought .... was the funniest when he...

I wish I was there when...

My top 5 fav **1D** moments:

1.

2.

3.

4.

5.

SAY WHAT?!?

The boys say the cutest things! Do you know which boy said what? Match the face to the words.

1. 'Just because you have the flaws, does not mean you aren't beautiful.'

2. 'We have a choice. To Live or To Exist.'

4. 'I don't know, it's odd that girls ask if they can hug me. Don't ask, do it. I'm just a regular guy.'

3. 'Before you judge people, judge yourself.'

5. 'Enjoy life, it has an expiration date.'

6. 'No matter how many times people try to criticize you, the best revenge is to prove them wrong.'

8. 'I think you have to take me for me. I am who I am.'

7. 'Live life for the moment because everything else is uncertain.'

10. 'Believe it or not, but even when I'm sleeping, I'm dreaming about meeting fans.'

9. 'I'll always defend the people I love.'

Check your answers on page 93.

DAYDREAM DIARY

Date: _____

I ♥
1D

Dear Diary,

My favourite daydream about 1D is...

_____

_____

_____

_____

_____

_____

_____

_____

_____

_____

_____

_____

_____

_____

_____

_____

I ♥ HARRY
ZAYN
NIALL
LOUIS
LIAM

MY TALENTS

The One Direction boys are obviously super-amazingly talented, but everyone has some talents up their sleeves, too — even if they're not so obvious, or still being perfected!

My main talent is:
_____
_____
_____

But I can also:

1. _____
2. _____
3. _____
4. _____
5. _____

I ♥ ONE DIRECTION

The talents I am still working on are:

1.
2.
3.
4.
5.

My most secret talent that no one else knows about is:

Shhhhh!!!!!

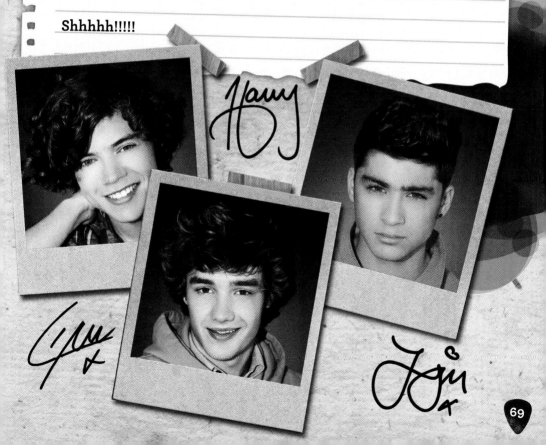

Ok, so if you absolutely HAD to write and star in a film with

One Direction, it would be:

Title:

Comedy | Romance | Action | Chick Flick | Science Fiction

This is how it would go...

Start

Middle

End

1D FAVS

There's something delicious about our favourite boys' favourite things!

The things you love say a lot about you. These cute favs give us little insights into what makes these boys tick.

FOOD

The bands' fav dessert — Cookies and Cream ice-cream!

Harry – loves Milky Way Crispy Rolls

Liam – loves Maltesers

Zayn – loves chicken

Louis – loves pizza

Niall – loves Asian food

Mine is: ....

COLOUR

Louis – dark red

Liam – purple

Niall – green

Harry – pink

Zayn – blue

Mine is: ....

FRAGRANCE

Liam – loves Paco Rabanne's 1 Million

Mine is: ....

SONGS FROM THE ALBUM

Harry – *More Than This*
Niall – *One Thing*
I love: ....

ANIMAL

Zayne – hammerhead sharks

Niall – giraffes

Liam – turtles

Mine is: ....

SPORT

Liam – basketball and boxing

I love: ....

POKEMON

Zayn – Oshawott

I love: ....

FILMS

Harry – *Love Actually* – awww
how sweet!!

Liam – *Toy Story* films – cute!

Louis – Grease

Mine is: ....

MUSIC

Harry ♥:
The Beatles, Cold Play,
Kings of Leon, Foster the People,
Shine On You Crazy Diamond
Pink Floyd

Niall ♥:
Swing music, including Frank
Sinatra, Dean Martin and
Michael Bublé
Rock music including The
Eagles, Bon Jovi and The Script

Zayn ♥:
Urban music, R&B and rap

Liam ♥:
Justin Timberlake
Gary Barlow from Take That
Somebody To Love is his fav
Justin Bieber song

Louis ♥:
Musicals
Robbie Williams
The Fray

I ♥ ....
....
....

MY GIRLZ

The **1D** boys shouldn't be the only ones to have fun travelling the world in a band with their best mates! There's nothing like a bit of girl power to rock the world. It's time to lay down your superstar plans for you and your besties.

When my bffs and I shoot to stardom...

Our band will be called:

Our stage names will be:

Our style of music will be:

Our fashion style will be:

It's going to be
Party time
★ awesome ★

Our first single will be called:

The concept behind the video will be:

The main cities we will tour in will be:

Our signature perfume will be called:

Introducing our band:

On vocals:

On drums:

On guitars:

MY ALBUM ART

Album cover art is made to get attention and express the ideas behind the music. Make your own covers by drawing, painting or sticking in cool images to make a collage. Get creative!

This is what I would have designed for the cover of *Up All Night*.

This is what I would design for the cover of my bands' first album.

BEING FAMOUS

Oh the hard life of the famous! Being flown around in a private jet, people bringing you whatever you want, sleeping all day until you have to go on stage ... it sounds really terrible! Best to be prepared for when fame strikes...

The best things about being famous would be ....

....

....

The worst things about being famous would be ....

....

....

With all my piles of money I would buy ....

....

....

I ♥ ONE DIRECTION

The charity I would donate the most to is ....
....
....

My celebrity best friend would be ....
....
....

The city I would live in most of the time is...............................
....
....

But I'd also have a house/apartment in ....
....
....

INTERVIEW ME!

If I was asked these questions by a magazine, I would say...

What do you love most about being famous?

What do you love least about being famous?

You've been on tour for a while, what's your favourite thing about going home?

What's your craziest tour story?

What's it like to travel the world with your best friends?

Where do you want to tour next?

What's your fav city?

What's your fav after-show snack?

Do you have any diva demands?

Who is your inspiration?

What band do you want to tour with the most?

DREAM HOLIDAY

I ♥ 1D

My dream holiday with One Direction would be:

☐ On an island
☑ In a glamorous city
☐ In the countryside
☐ At the beach
☐ Camping
☐ Other

I would pack:

I wouldn't leave without:

The friends I would take are:

I would want to go by:
- [ ] Plane
- [ ] Jet
- [ ] Car
- [✓] Helicopter
- [ ] Yacht
- [ ] Speedboat
- [ ] Train
- [ ] All of the above.

SWOON ALERT!

Country style!
A well-deserved
break for the boys
in the countryside.

Smile for
the camera!
Looking smart
casual for an
outdoor
photoshoot.

The beautiful boys working it for the camera.

Swoon-worthy smiles from all of the boys!

JUST MESSIN'

Photoshoots require a lot of hanging around behind the scenes.

So cute seeing the boys testing out their poses!

I ♥ ONE DIRECTION

Nautical suits them as they share a secret joke on the pier between shots.

Fooling around for another awesome photo opportunity!

MY 1D PARTY

Make your next party or sleepover a **1D** themed party. Follow these cool tips to make it a memorable one!

Food

Delicious food is very important. Make sure there are some healthy options and check if anyone has a food allergy before the party.

Try some of the **1D** boys' most-loved dishes, like Cookies and Cream ice-cream, for dessert. Mmmmmm!

Decorations

Get everyone to bring their favourite posters and pics of the band and stick them up all over the room (with your parents' or guardians' permission, of course!)

Music

Obviously, the band of the night will be on the playlist. But to mix it up a little, cut up some scraps of paper and get everyone to write down their fav **1D** track. Count up the votes in secret then play your guests' choices in order so you end with everyone's fav song at number 1! Now you know which song your bffs love the most, make up a dance to go along with it. It's a good excuse to play your fav song on repeat!

Games

Give classic games a 1D twist! For example, for a 1D pass-the-parcel, add a note with a question on each layer, such as 'Which band member said that he loves Maltesers?' When the music stops, the person with the parcel has to answer the question correctly to be able to open the layer. Or if they get it wrong, they could choose a truth or dare option! Make the final present inside a cute 1D gift.

Thank You

Take loads of pics of your bffs throughout the party. Afterwards you can print the pics and write nice notes on the back to thank everyone for coming and making it a great time!

ONE DIRECTION

It's going to be

Have fun!

★ awesome ★

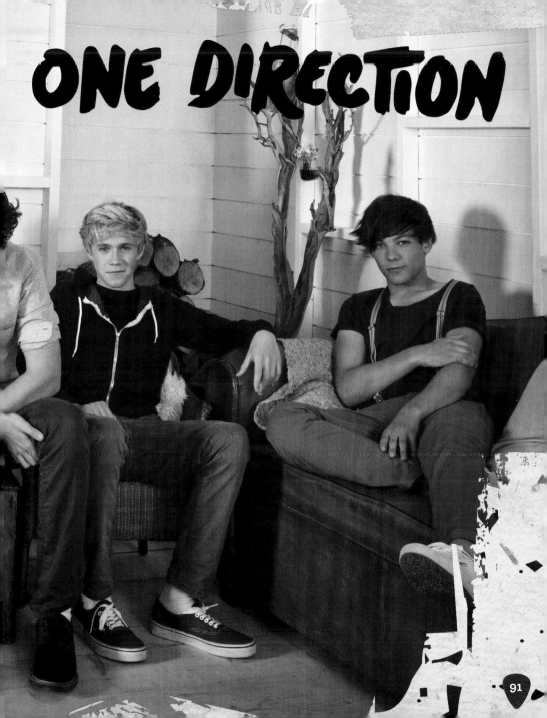

ONE DIRECTION

91

I  1D

Harry

Liam

Louis x

Niall

Zayn x

ANSWERS

Page 21

1. *Tell Me A Lie*
2. *More Than This, Taken,* **and** *Stole My Heart*
3. *Thirteen*

Page 36

B	E	A	U	T	I	F	U	L	C	R	T	X	E	P
F	V	S	E	P	H	O	H	P	E	H	A	F	M	O
E	D	V	Y	X	Y	S	N	N	Z	P	K	A	A	P
X	O	N	C	S	U	I	O	E	K	F	E	C	F	N
L	E	R	A	C	T	I	K	B	T	L	N	T	N	D
J	K	F	C	B	T	N	H	F	Z	H	E	O	Q	A
J	V	E	L	C	L	X	E	F	P	I	I	R	H	H
X	S	Z	E	L	X	Z	M	M	P	M	E	N	L	N
S	Z	R	I	S	Z	Y	M	K	O	V	H	L	G	F
Z	I	A	S	D	N	E	I	R	F	M	A	B	Y	M
D	M	Y	G	R	H	S	L	L	F	I	N	Y	A	Z
G	Y	D	N	A	J	B	X	O	N	U	F	Q	J	Q
C	S	E	I	W	B	O	Y	S	U	Z	N	O	R	E
T	O	O	W	A	H	A	R	R	Y	I	V	D	V	G
H	E	W	Z	U	Z	V	M	M	K	B	S	J	G	I

Page 38

Possible answers: ride, nine, dire, none, nerd, tire, red, rode, done, neon, direct, drone, cite, tree

Page 42

1. Niall and Liam
2. Harry
3. Harry
4. Tell Me A Lie
5. Zayn
6. Arabic
7. Left
8. Edward

Page 43

1. b)
2. a)
3. a)
4. b)
5. b)
6. a)
7. c)

1D FAVS

There's something delicious about our favourite boys' favourite things!

The things you love say a lot about you. These cute favs give us little insights into what makes these boys tick.

FOOD

The bands' fav dessert – Cookies and Cream ice-cream!

Harry – loves Milky Way Crispy Rolls

Liam – loves Maltesers

Zayn – loves chicken

Louis – loves pizza

Niall – loves Asian food

Mine is: ....

COLOUR

Louis – dark red

Liam – purple

Niall – green

Harry – pink

Zayn – blue

Mine is: ....

FRAGRANCE

Liam – loves Paco Rabanne's 1 Million

Mine is: ....

SONGS FROM THE ALBUM

Harry – *More Than This*

Niall – *One Thing*

I love: ....

Middle

End